P9-DFK-745

God's Hall of Fame

Ellyn Sanna

BARBOUR
PUBLISHING, INC.
Uhrichsville, Ohio

© MCMXCVIII by Barbour Publishing, Inc.

ISBN 1-57748-428-2

Published by Barbour Publishing, Inc., P.O. Box 719, Uhrichsville, OH 44683 http://www.barbourbooks.com

Member of the
Evangelical Christian
Publishers Association

Printed in the United States of America.

CONTENTS

INTRODUCTION

The differences between the men and women in this book are significant, at least on the surface. Some had powerful intellects and impressive résumés, while others lacked any formal education whatsoever. Some were great reformers who started religious movements that changed the shape of Christianity, while others lived their lives quietly, in complete submission to the church of their day. Many of these men and women lived dramatic lives of danger and excitement, while others did nothing more remarkable than work in a kitchen or wonder at a handful of snow.

The lesson we learn from their differences is that God is not limited by our culture or our talents or any other circumstance of our lives. He does not work in one prescribed way. Instead, His Spirit moves powerfully throughout the world He created, using everyone and everything.

And that is the one thing these men and women had in common, the one thing that earned them their reputations: Each was totally and absolutely open to the Spirit of God. They were neither perfect nor were they limp, bloodless saints, but their lives were completely focused on Jesus Christ.

God used that focus in a variety of ways. Some were called to minister to physical needs and others to spiritual needs, but all of them changed our world in some way as they allowed the Holy Spirit to work through them. They were God's body, powerfully at work in His creation.

In *Techniques of Fiction,* Leon Sumerlian says, "The saint should be dangerous—more dangerous than the sinner. He should live dangerously, as in the past. The saint should not be a weakling or some spectral spirit." The women and men in this book were dangerous people, for they disturbed the status quo forever.

As we read their stories, may we find that they are just as dangerous now as ever, for their stories have the power to challenge us, shaking the foundations of our safe, complacent lives.

AUGUSTINE
SHAPER OF THE FAITH

Then Jesus said, ". . . Let me teach you,
because I am humble and gentle,
and you will find rest for your souls."
MATTHEW 11:28–29

The men and women whose lives are described in this book are like links in a chain, each one building on the legacy of faith that has been left to them by the ones who came before. An even more fitting metaphor might be a net, or a web of interconnecting strands. The metaphor the Bible uses is a living body, with each member necessary to the health of the entire organism. Augustine not only comes first in this book alphabetically, but he also comes first chronologically: Those who came later built on the foundation that he had laid. He brought to his faith a brilliant and logical mind, and left behind a thorough and deeply spiritual theology. Almost 1600 years later, his thoughts continue to shape the Christian world.

Augustine was born in A.D. 354 in North Africa, which was then part of the decaying Roman Empire. His father, though not wealthy, was a Roman administrator of their village. His mother, Monica, who had been converted to Christianity, was an intensely spiritual woman. Undoubtedly, her influence was immense in her son's life.

Monica taught her son about Christianity when he was a child, but when he was eleven or twelve, he was sent away from home to study grammar and literature at a school twenty miles away. Although while there he grew away from her Christian influence, his mother's early teaching remained dormant in his heart, whispering to him of something he lacked, no matter how well he did at his studies.

When he was sixteen his father sent him to school in Carthage, hoping that he would become a lawyer. He was a quiet, studious young man who enjoyed philosophy and academics. He found his deepest pleasure in the world of books and writing, and when he completed his studies, he decided to become a man of letters rather than follow his father's ambition for him. A gifted writer, Augustine won a prize for his poetry and he wrote his first book when he was in his early twenties.

During this time Augustine was influenced by the Manicheans, a sect that believed physical matter was evil. Unlike Christianity, which affirms the holiness of the physical world through the incarnation of Christ, the Manicheans believed that the human spirit must be released from physical matter if it is to find goodness. For a time Augustine believed he had found the answers to life in this philosophy, but eventually the Manicheans no longer satisfied him. He sank into doubt and agnosticism. His heart became restless, seeking a spiritual home.

He accepted a municipal chair of rhetoric in the city of Milan and there he met Ambrose, a leader of the church. Augustine's friendship with Ambrose eventually led him to the answers to his heart's longing and he converted to Christianity in 386. He wrote about his long spiritual and philosophical journey in his most famous book, *Confessions*. After becoming a Christian, Augustine decided to return to Africa and live a quiet, solitary life of prayer and study. He sold all his property and gave the proceeds to the poor, then retired from society.

God had other plans for Augustine, however. In 391, despite Augustine's protests, the Bishop of Hippo ordained him into the priesthood. Augustine left his lonely, quiet life and began preaching to the congregation in Hippo. His sermons were based directly on the Scriptures, and the people valued them so much that they transcribed his words as he spoke. Today, Christians still learn from these commentaries on the Bible.

Augustine also began a long series of public disputes with the African heretics. These discussions continued throughout the rest of Augustine's life. With his gift of words, Augustine used this public forum to express his faith—and the Holy Spirit used Augustine, convincing many people of the truth about Christ.

Four or five years later Augustine was called to accept what he called "the burden of the episcopate." For the next thirty-five years, all his energy was spent defending and promoting the Church in northern Africa. Christianity was a young enough faith that its doctrine was still being shaped, and Augustine's influence was important in many councils and conferences that dealt with various heresies.

In 426 Augustine retired, upon arranging for his successor as Bishop of Hippo. But his best-laid plans to spend his time writing, revising, and correcting the doctrine in the works he had already written were not to be. At the time of his retirement North Africa was involved in a civil war against Rome. Vandals from Spain helped in the fight against the imperial forces, and in 430 the Roman army was defeated. The army sought refuge in Hippo, where they were pursued by the vandal army. Augustine died when the siege was in its third month.

Although he died in the midst of such tumult, he went home to God in peace, his heart at rest. As Augustine wrote in his *Confessions,* "Thou hast made us for Thyself, O God, and our heart is restless until it finds its rest in Thee."

RECOMMENDED READING: *Confessions* and *City of God* by Augustine

EVANGELINE BOOTH
MILITANT HOLINESS

*God's discipline is always right and good for us
because it means we will share in his holiness.*
HEBREWS 12:10

In the nineteenth century the holiness movement gained widespread acceptance. The movement was based on two premises: The grace of Christ on the Cross is the only cure for humanity's broken sinfulness, and second, after conversion our sinful tendencies continue, but God offers us perfection through grace as His love heals the last remnants of our selfishness. Among the many religious organizations spawned by the holiness movement was the Salvation Army, a group whose members pledged themselves to lives of holy love while they fought to win others for Christ. This distinctly military outlook has characterized the Salvation Army since its inception.

During the early twentieth century Evangeline Booth commanded the Salvation Army in the United States. She was a woman of fire, charm, and grace who was dedicated to her Lord and His business on earth.

The fourth daughter of Catherine and William Booth, the original founders of the Salvation Army, Evangeline grew up in the midst of a hectic household where she was encouraged to be strong-willed and dramatic. Her father looked on her as a sort of princess, an heir to the throne, and thus, as a young woman she was placed in positions where she had authority over thousands, answering to no one except God and her father.

In most cases, her father trusted her to God.

Evangeline was thirty-nine when her father gave her command of the United States branch of the Salvation Army. A mixture of vanity and dedication, and charm and haughtiness, she had a genuine burden for the poor yet she could also be condescending. She was not perfect, but she was dedicated to God and His work, and He used her, despite her flaws.

Evangeline Booth had many gifts to offer God. When it came to evangelism, she was fearless. She was also a gifted administrator, with the ability to keep many details in focus. Her compassion extended to her subordinates also; people liked to work for her. She had an unusual sense of humor that helped people see that the serious business of evangelism can be filled with play-ful joy. And most of all, she was a gifted speaker who could hold large audiences enthralled for hours at a time. Her speaking talents were just as powerful in private settings, too, as she was skilled at persuading rich men to donate large sums of money to the Salvation Army. God used all of her talents to help the Salvation Army grow into a flourishing and productive church in the United States.

Evangeline Booth was "promoted to Glory" in 1950 at the age of eighty-four. One biographer says of her, "She had done all that a leader could do to make the Salvation Army strong and popular in the United States. She had been proud of Christ, proud of the Army, proud of the uniform, and proud of the poor and lonely people that mostly filled the ranks behind her; they sensed that pride and returned it with love. The

Commander left behind her a legacy of high courage, of zeal, of kindness, of caprice. . . . She filled the Army with excitement, and gave it a sense of high purpose. She loved people for loving her, and for their souls' sakes."

Despite her foibles, Evangeline Booth submitted to God's discipline, and she shared in His holiness. Her secret, she once told a reporter, was this: "I live for others. My deepest desire is to make every person I meet a little better because I have passed this way."

RECOMMENDED READING: *The General Was a Lady: The Story of Evangeline Booth* by Margaret Troutt (A.J. Holman Co.)

JOHN BUNYAN
GOD'S PILGRIM

*They were looking for a better place,
a heavenly homeland. That is why God
is not ashamed to be called their God,
for he has prepared a heavenly city for them.*
HEBREWS 11:16

John Bunyan's life shines with grace. While he lacked what the world recognizes as important, such as education and wealth, he committed to God the gifts he did possess: a genius for the English language and a childlike imagination. Bunyan's fifty-five books, which uniquely describe the work of redemption, are still read 300 years later by Christians the world over. Despite sorrows and worldly troubles, doubts and spiritual anguish, Bunyan continued to yield his genius to God, allowing the Holy Spirit to use his talents to the fullest.

John Bunyan was born in 1628, in the village of Elstow, near Bedford, in the Midlands of England, and he married for the first time when he was nineteen. The name of this wife is unknown today, but without her John Bunyan would not have been the same man. Although she was a poor woman, her "dowry," Bunyan would later write, was more precious than gold. She told him stories of her father, a man who had loved God in a way that challenged Bunyan to take a new look at his own life, and she gave him two books that had enormous influence on him. These books opened up for Bunyan the spiritual and literary pathways he was to follow for his entire life.

Like many other women of her day, his wife did not live to be thirty. She died in 1658, leaving behind four children. Eventually, Bunyan married again. His new wife, Elizabeth, was as strong a woman as his first wife, and she was faithful both to her husband and to God all through Bunyan's long imprisonment.

That imprisonment would never have happened if Bunyan had not begun to take his faith so seriously. He had been raised in the Church of England, a moderate, middle-of-the-road sort of upbringing, and as an adolescent his religion meant little to him. He was selfish and shallow, more interested in having a good time than in thoughts of divine love. His first wife's influence, though, had begun to change him, and God continued the work after her death.

Conversion was neither short nor easy for Bunyan and for years he was filled with doubts and despair. Like the hero Christian of his most famous story, *The Pilgrim's Progress,* his life was an ongoing pilgrimage. Perhaps his humility kept him from ever feeling he had "arrived" in his walk with God. Nonetheless, he clearly saw the Christian life as a journey, a road filled with darkness and trouble as well as light and joy, a road that we must travel our whole life until we reach our heavenly homeland in the world to come.

Several milestones stand out in Bunyan's pilgrimage. The first demonstrates that God uses the most unlikely people to bring the Spirit's conviction to others. In Bunyan's own words, "One day as I was standing at a neighbor's shop window, cursing and swearing and playing the madman as I was so apt to do, the woman who sat inside heard me." This woman was not a particularly moral person; in fact, Bunyan describes her life as "loose and ungodly." Still, she was offended by Bunyan's language and behavior and she reminded him that he was influencing the other young people in the village. Her words pricked Bunyan's conscience; he hung his head, secretly ashamed, and wished that he could start his life over again, a clean innocent child with no bad habits to break.

At that point in his life he could not conceive that he could be anything other than what he was: a frivolous, lying, foulmouthed young man. But soon after he became friends with a poor man who truly lived his religion and who, in Bunyan's words, "talked pleasantly of the Scriptures." Through this man's influence, Bunyan began to study the Bible and "began to take pleasure in reading it."

Another milestone in Bunyan's conversion occurred later, and this time the Spirit worked in his life through the ordinary conversation of several poor women, a conversation that was not even directed at Bunyan but that he overheard as he was walking down the streets of Bedford. Bunyan wrote later that these women were talking about "a new birth, the work of God on their hearts. . . . They also talked how God visited their souls with His love in the Lord Jesus, and with what words and promises they had been refreshed, comforted, and supported. . . . And I thought they spoke as if joy did make them speak; they spoke with such pleasantness of Scripture language, and with such appearance of grace in all they said, that they were to me as if they had found a new world."

Bunyan tore himself away and went on down the street, but these women's conversation stayed with him. Later, in a dream about them, Bunyan imagined he at last had found his way into the "new world" he had glimpsed, a world of sunlight and joy. "This vision lived in my thoughts for many days," wrote Bunyan, "and during all this time I saw myself as being a sad, forlorn creature—and yet I had an insistent, serious hunger to be one of those who sat in the sunshine. I began to pray wherever I was, whether at home or away, in the house or out in the field; and I would find myself often singing the Fifty-first Psalm, with my heart suddenly lifting. . ."

Again, history does not record the names of these women whose conversation had such an influence on Bunyan. Bunyan himself may never have known their names. And yet because these women sat in the sun one day talking of God and His mercy, Bunyan's life was changed forever—and because his life was changed, thousands of other people have been touched by God's Spirit through Bunyan's writings down through the centuries.

Eventually, Bunyan became a Puritan, a decision that put him into conflict with the government of his day. As a result, he was arrested for preaching his views on redemption; if he had promised to quit preaching, he would have been soon released, but Bunyan refused to make that promise. His imprisonment lasted twelve years. During this time he missed his wife and children and he worried about their well-being. Despite his fears and longings, however, he used this time both to grow in his knowledge of God and to write thirteen of his works.

If God can use prison and poverty to His glory in John Bunyan's life, He can certainly use whatever trials we face today. God has an amazing economy that wastes nothing. Even our fears and doubts can be put to use for His kingdom, if we only commit ourselves totally and absolutely to His Spirit.

Throughout his life Bunyan was never immune to doubt. The Puritans were intensely Calvinistic, believing in the doctrine of election (or predestination). Although they emphasized the importance of grace, they also lapsed frequently into discouragement and fear. What if you were not one of the elect after all? How could you know for certain that God had predestined you for heaven? What if you had missed the "day of grace"—in other words, what if God had called you when you weren't listening, and now He would never call again? Questions like these tormented John Bunyan.

During the early years of his faith he was preoccupied with an almost neurotic obsession that he was not saved after all, swinging back and forth between hope and despair. His writings record this experience, a back-and-forth rhythm between joyous faith and selfish preoccupation that reads like the Old Testament account of God's dealings with His people, the Israelites. Despite the Israelites' doubts and selfishness, God calls them back again and again with unending love and patience.

If we are honest, most of us will recognize our own ongoing conversion in Bunyan's descriptions of the on-again, off-again nature of human faith. His unflinching accounts of the human pilgrimage comfort our own self-doubts. Surely we are not the only ones who have been fickle in our love for God: Three hundred years ago Bunyan experienced the same trials we do today. And then as now, God's love endures; He seeks us out over and over and over, using whatever means He can, healing our faithlessness, bringing us back to Himself. We may swing back and forth, but in Him there is no shadow of turning.

By the time Bunyan lay dying at the age of fifty-nine, his fears had apparently disappeared forever. Like one of his characters in *The Pilgrim's Progress,* he was calm and joyful as he ventured into death's darkness. He had spent his entire life absorbing the Bible, and now as much as ever, its words and wisdom spilled out as he talked with his family, quoting Scripture after Scripture that speaks of the joy to come after death. The worries and neurotic anxiety that had troubled him through so much of his life were gone.

After he and his family prayed together, he told them, "It's all right for you to cry and feel sad—but don't cry for me. I am going to the Father of our Lord Jesus Christ. Even though I am a sinner, He will welcome me home. Before long, we will all be singing a new song together. And then we will be happy forever and ever—world without end." John Bunyan went home to the heavenly city God had prepared for him.

RECOMMENDED READING: *The Riches of Bunyan: Selections from the Writings of John Bunyan,* updated in today's language by Ellyn Sanna, and *The Pilgrim's Progress* by John Bunyan (both from Barbour Publishing, Inc.)

WILLIAM CAREY
GREAT THINGS FOR GOD

*May the Lord bring you into an
ever deeper understanding of the love of God
and the endurance that comes from Christ.*
2 THESSALONIANS 3:5

God makes use of whatever we give Him. Even those qualities that seem of little value to ourselves, when we put them in God's hands can be used to His glory. William Carey (1761–1834) was an ordinary person with one extraordinary talent: a gift for languages. He also possessed a dogged determination to stick to any task to which he put his hand. Like the small lunch of loaves and fish that Christ multiplied to feed thousands, God multiplied the morsels of talent and strength in Carey's character and used them to reach thousands for His kingdom.

William Carey was born into a working-class home in England. His parents were unusual in that they not only owned a Bible, but they read it regularly to their children. The value of reading and the value of Scripture were impressed on Carey from the time he was a child.

As a teenager his fascination with language continued, and while apprenticed as a shoemaker, he learned Latin, Hebrew, French, Greek, and Dutch. Even though he could read the Bible in six different languages, his interest in the Scriptures was purely academic at this point. In his own words, he was "addicted to swearing, lying, and unchaste conversation."

About this time, though, another apprentice who worked with Carey, a young man named John Warr, began to talk to Carey about an experiential knowledge of God. Warr was a member of a group called the Dissenters, nonconformists who were at odds with England's established church. While Carey was not impressed with them or their views, his discussions with Warr began to change Carey's life.

Just as He did in John Bunyan's life, God used the fresh views of a religious movement outside the mainline, established church to work in Carey's heart. At a Dissenters' meeting, upon hearing a young man speak these words as his text, "Let us go forth therefore unto him without the camp, bearing his reproach," Carey responded by surrendering himself to God and His kingdom.

Shortly after that Carey began preaching the Gospel himself. One day a friend stopped him and rebuked him for neglecting his business. "Neglecting my business!" Carey answered. "My business is to extend the Kingdom of God; I only cobble shoes to pay expenses."

Eventually, Carey's commitment to the Gospel led him to India. Throughout his time there he reached out to the lowest castes, spreading the message that even the humblest person, the person whom all others have rejected, may trust in God. After all, the Christ who was put to death "without the camp" was the Christ who had first brought Carey to surrender to grace.

While in India, Carey was appalled by the practice of suttee, where a living widow is burned to death with her dead husband. After seeing a young woman put to death this way, Carey committed his life to bringing an end to this practice. He knew that the Christ who had died as an outsider, rejected by the world, was the same Christ who loved these women deemed expendable by their culture. Carey felt Christ's pain for these sacrificed lives and, after thirty-three years, he was finally successful in bringing about the reform that put an end to suttee.

Besides his gift for languages, Carey was useful to the Spirit because of his ability to keep going, year after year, in the face of apparent failure. When fire destroyed the building that contained his printing press, as well as all his manuscripts, grammars, and dictionaries—Carey had worked for years to translate the Bible into the language of the people—he did not react with despair, impatience, or anger. Instead, he simply knelt and thanked God that he still had the strength and ability to do the work all over again.

In his second letter to the Thessalonians, the apostle Paul links endurance with the love of God, implying that the two are somehow tied together. But most of us never realize just how powerful a trait endurance can be. Carey himself never placed much value on such a characteristic, although he understood that, as water wears away stone, so the ability to keep going in the end accomplishes great things. He once explained himself to his nephew: "I can plod. That is my only genius. I can persevere in any definite pursuit. To this I owe everything." Acknowledging that the word plod comes from an old Middle English word that means "a puddle," one of Carey's biographers commented, "A 'plodder' is someone who is willing to get his feet wet and wade through water to get to his destination. He keeps going."

Another of Carey's biographers, A. T. Pierson, said this of his subject: "With little teaching, he became learned; poor himself, he made millions rich." Indeed, William Carey lived his entire life by this saying: "Attempt great things for God, expect great things from God."

RECOMMENDED READING: *William Carey* by Russell Olt (Warner Press)

AMY CARMICHAEL
AN ORDINARY WOMAN WITH EXTRAORDINARY LOVE

God is love,
and all who live in love live in God,
and God lives in them.
1 JOHN 4:16

Many Christians are more comfortable if they can fit themselves and others into some denominational slot. Amy Carmichael, however, refused to accept any such label. When a boy she raised was asked what kind of Christian he was, he was totally mystified. "I am just a Christian!" he replied. Amy had taught him that the Christian faith should hold no pigeonholes; we are all one in Christ, and following Christ does not mean believing one doctrine over another, or following this practice instead of that. Instead, it means simply loving as Christ loved.

Amy Carmichael was born in Ireland in 1867 to parents who were strictly religious. They expected their children to sit quietly, without moving or speaking, through long church services. Thus Amy early learned the meaning of discipline, and also the importance of total, unswerving commitment to Christ.

When she grew up she felt called to the mission field. She responded with joy and went first to Japan and then China and Ceylon, finally ending up in India where she founded the Dohnavur Fellowship, a refuge for children. She spent fifty-three years there, never taking a furlough back to Europe, immersing herself in the Indian way of life. Like the other great missionaries in this book, Amy understood that the message of Christ transcends cultures. At Dohnavur Fellowship meat was never served so that the vegetarian Hindus would not be offended. Furthermore, Amy herself always wore saris and did the menial jobs of the lowest castes. She died in India when she was eighty-four.

Her dedication to God was amazing and unshakable, but Amy was no more perfect than any other human being. She never saw herself as anything but an ordinary, practical person, as common and earthy as a potato. That was her metaphor for herself. Another time she described herself as a "slug on a cabbage leaf." She was famous for her temper, and apologies were next to impossible for her.

Despite that, she was obsessed with treating others with the respect they deserved. Those who worked in her house were never allowed to speak negatively of someone who was not present. In fact, a sign hung above the dining room table, "May the absent one be always safe at our table!" Such a philosophy sprang from a challenge given her early in her missionary career. While she was in Japan, a Japanese woman was startled by the backbiting between the missionaries there. "Can you show us the love of your Lord Jesus?" the woman asked, and her question echoed in Amy's heart for the rest of her life.

The principle which governed her life—"Ask not how little but how much can love give"—gave her the power to carry Christ to those who needed Him. "When she hugged me," said a woman who had known her, "all my burdens went away!"

Elisabeth Elliot wrote of Amy Carmichael's challenge to us today: "Will we be put off by her awesome discipline, her steadfastness, or perhaps by the cultural shift or the difference in vocabulary? She spoke often of the 'country whose forces move unseen among us.' That country is our country. We are its citizens as she was, if we call ourselves Christians. If its forces moved in Dohnavur, they move unabated here, too, where we live. If we are unaware, perhaps we have not listened, taken time to observe."

In Amy's own words, "He, Who loved you unto death, is speaking to you. Listen, do not be deaf and blind to Him. And as you keep quiet and listen, you will know, deep down in your heart, that you are loved. As the air is around you, so is His love around about you now. Trust that love to guide your lives. It will never, never fail."

Her whole life, this was Amy's prayer: "Lord, do Thou turn me all into love."

RECOMMENDED READING: *A Chance to Die: The Life and Legacy of Amy Carmichael* by Elisabeth Elliot (Revell)

BIDDY (MRS. OSWALD) CHAMBERS
AN INVISIBLE WOMAN

I myself no longer live,
but Christ lives in me.
GALATIANS 2:20

The name Biddy Chambers is not well-known. We do not know how this woman came to Christ or what she was like. We know very little about her except that she was a wife and mother, who before her marriage worked as a stenographer. However, the world does remember the name of her husband, Oswald Chambers, the well-known and much-loved devotional writer. Biddy Chambers undoubtedly had private ambitions, personal gifts, and secret weaknesses, but we do not know what they were. She lived in a day when a wife's accomplishments were not as important as her husband's. And yet her humble surrender to God made her essential to the work of His kingdom.

Oswald Chambers worked with the British troops in Egypt in connection with the YMCA. Throughout her husband's ministry, Biddy sat quietly in his congregation, taking notes on her husband's messages, her hand flying as she used the shorthand at which she had become so skilled when she was a stenographer. She took hundreds of pages of notes.

In 1917 Oswald Chambers died at age forty-three from complications following an appendectomy. Biddy was only thirty-four, alone in a foreign country with a young daughter, but apparently possessed of an unshakable faith. She sent a telegram to their family and friends at home that read simply, "OSWALD IN HIS PRESENCE."

Biddy returned home to England and began putting her husband's many sermons, recorded in her notes, into book form. She had enough material for fifty books, all of which bear her husband's name but only her initials. The most well known of these is *My Utmost for His Highest.*

Without Biddy, Oswald Chambers would have been recognized as a gifted speaker whose influence was limited to the British soldiers he served in Egypt at the beginning of the twentieth century. Because of her, however, Oswald Chambers's influence continues to be felt in God's kingdom, and his words continue to inspire us to give all that we have and are to God. Her prayer, wrote Biddy, was that "day by day the messages may continue to bring the quickening life and inspiration of the Holy Spirit."

Biddy's prayer has been answered. She put little importance on her own life but allowed Christ to live in her. Her total surrender to God earned her a place in His hall of fame.

RECOMMENDED READING: *Oswald Chambers: Abandoned to God* by David McCasland (Discovery House Publishers)

FANNY CROSBY
GOD'S SONGWRITER

He has given me a new song to sing,
a hymn of praise to our God.
PSALM 40:3

Sometimes we feel we have nothing to offer God. We may be handicapped by shyness, emotional pain, or physical disabilities. And yet if we open ourselves to the Spirit's power, God can use us, just as He used a blind woman named Fanny Crosby.

Fanny Crosby was born in the United States during the first half of the nineteenth century. When she was six weeks old, a doctor made a tragic mistake that left her permanently blind. Later that year, before her first birthday, her father died.

Perhaps as a result of these tragedies, Fanny grew up to be so neurotically shy that she never spoke out loud in public. She had some musical ability, however, and on the condition that she never be called on to speak, she played the piano for Christian meetings at the blind institution where she attended.

At these meetings she met a young man, a Mr. Camp, who was able to break through her shyness. They became good friends and, all her life, Fanny attributed her conversion to this young man, though he never actually did anything to persuade her to open her life to God. Instead, the Spirit used a dream to speak to Fanny. In her autobiography, Fanny described the dream this way:

"It seemed that the sky had been cloudy for a

number of days, and finally someone came to me and said that Mr. Camp desired to see me at once. Then I thought I entered the room and found him very ill.

" 'Fanny,' he asked, 'will you meet me in Heaven?'

" 'Yes, I will, God helping me,' I replied; and I thought his last words were, 'Remember you promised a dying man!' Then the clouds seem to roll from my spirit and I awoke. I could not forget those words, 'Will you meet me in Heaven?' and although my friend was perfectly well, I began to consider whether I could really meet him or any other acquaintance in the Better Land. . . ."

The dream continued to haunt Fanny's thoughts, just as John Bunyan's dream had haunted him two centuries earlier. Once again the Holy Spirit was at work, persuading someone to yield her talents to Him for His use.

At last, while Fanny was attending revival meetings at a Methodist church, she was able to conquer her shyness enough to go forward all alone at the end of the meeting. The congregation was singing a hymn, and when they reached the line, "Lord, I give myself away," Fanny felt as though her soul was flooded with light. This timid woman, who had never before spoken out loud in public, sprang to her feet and shouted, "Hallelujah!" Later that week, she stood up at a class meeting and promised to do whatever God made clear to her that He wanted.

A few weeks later she was asked to close her class meetings with a prayer. Her first thought was, *I can't*— but then she remembered her promise. Choking back her fear, she stood and prayed out loud. After that, she said, a block seemed to have been removed from her life, allowing her to be blessed over and over as she passed her blessings on to others.

When she was forty-four she began writing hymns. Before she died at the age of ninety-five, she had written over 9,000 hymns, more than anyone in the history of Christianity. Some of her best-loved works were composed in less than an hour. Often on very short notice she would be asked to listen to a tune and then frame words to fit the music. One day a man hurried into her house and said, "Fanny, in forty minutes I must catch the train to Cincinnati, and I need a new song for a great Sunday school convention there." The two of them discussed the sort of song that was needed, and then he glanced at his watch. "Thirty minutes left, Fanny." She turned to her desk and then soon handed him a piece of paper. On it were the words to what many think is her greatest hymn, "Safe in the Arms of Jesus."

Although she was blind her whole life, many of her hymns refer to the sight that she was confident would be hers one day in heaven. For example, consider this line from "Blessed Assurance":

Visions of rapture now burst on my sight.

Or lines like,

Oh, the soul-thrilling rapture when I view His
blessed face. . .

I know I shall see in His beauty the King. . .

Once Fanny Crosby opened herself up to God, He changed her from a neurotically shy girl into a creative, self-confident woman who dedicated her talents to God's kingdom. She had no doubt that one day she would see Him face-to-face, and tell the story—"Saved by Grace."

RECOMMENDED READING: *Memories of Eighty Years* by Fanny Crosby (Hodder & Stoughton)

JIM ELLIOT
MARTYR FOR CHRIST

For we know that when this earthly tent
we live in is taken down—
when we die and leave these bodies—
we will have a home in heaven,
an eternal body made for us by God himself.
2 CORINTHIANS 5:1

When we make a commitment to Christ, few of us today expect to give up everything, indeed to die, for our faith. Jim Elliot's life calls us to examine our Christianity, to see if it measures up to the standard he set. As he wrote in college, "He is no fool who gives what he cannot keep to gain what he cannot lose." That statement proved to be prophetic, as Elliot would give his mortal life for the sake of Christ, entering into life eternal. Are we too absorbed in keeping what we know we'll lose. . .and not focused enough on giving?

Jim Elliot, born in 1927, was from Portland, Oregon. He attended Wheaton College in Wheaton, Illinois, where he was the president of the Student Mission Fellowship. A few years later, while working in the jungles of Ecuador, Jim married Elisabeth Howard, whom he had met at Wheaton and who was also involved in the mission field.

Again and again Jim had heard about the feared Auca Indians, an Ecuadorian Stone Age tribe that had a reputation for being killers, a tribe that had never warmed to the gestures of white people, soldiers or missionaries. Together with four other men—Nate Saint,

Ed McCully, Roger Youderian, and Pete Fleming—Jim began to feel burdened for the Aucas, as though God were calling him to carry the Gospel to these people.

The first missionary to enter Auca land, a Jesuit priest, had been murdered in 1667. For 200 years white people had avoided the Aucas—until the rubber hunters came, and then later the oil companies. These mercenaries murdered and looted, raped and burned, and the Indians fought back with the deadliest means they could find. Other Europeans continued to stay as far away from them as they could.

But Jim Elliot and his friends knew that Christ loved these people, and they longed to share the Good News with them. Nate Saint had made the acquaintance of a young Auca girl who worked for a local landowner, and she began teaching him useful words and phrases in the Auca language. Meanwhile, the others made plans to fly over the Auca land and drop gifts in a bucket reeled up and down from the plane by telephone wire.

The day came when they felt that it was the Lord's time for them to move ahead. The men began dropping gifts as they had planned, while they called from a loudspeaker Auca phrases they had learned: "We like you! We like you! We have come to visit you." The people on the ground took the gifts. After a while, they began to smile and wave at the airplane; eventually, they put return gifts in the drop bucket.

At last in January 1956 the missionaries met for a final prayer meeting. Together they sang a favorite hymn:

We rest on Thee, our Shield and Defender;
Thine is the battle, Thine shall be the praise;
When passing through the gates of pearly splendor
Victors, we rest with Thee through endless days.

Then the men said good-bye to their wives and headed into the Auca jungle.

During the next few days the women heard from their husbands over the radio. On the fifth day, Marj Saint spoke with her husband in the morning. He told her that a commission of ten men would be meeting with them. "Pray for us," he told her. "This is the day!" Arranging to talk with her again later that afternoon, he signed off.

But the wives received no more messages. The following day another missionary pilot spotted their plane, stripped of all its fabric. He saw no sign of the five men. Obviously, something was wrong. A search party was sent out to find them.

Word spread around the world that five missionaries were missing in Ecuador. People everywhere were praying. The Air Force sent out planes—and found the men's speared bodies adrift in the Curaray River.

Christians all over the world were stunned. How could God have let this happen? The five men's deaths seemed so pointless. They had died before they accomplished anything. How could their deaths serve God's kingdom?

And yet ripples spread out from this tragedy, changing the lives of people everywhere. *Life* magazine covered the Auca massacre and, as a result, people across America heard about missions and the Gospel. People in crisis situations remembered the words of Jim Elliot that *Life* had quoted—"When it comes time to die, make sure that all you have to do is die"—and his words transformed their lives. Others felt called to give their lives to God so that they could step into the empty places left by the five missionaries. In the years after the massacre, missions were flooded with offers from people who wanted to "take the place" of the martyrs.

The ripples that spread from their deaths were strongest, of course, in their own families. Their wives and children could have been bitter; they could have turned from God. Instead, four of them returned to work with the Auca Indians. A month after the massacre Nate's sister, Rachel Saint, and Elisabeth Elliot went to live with the Aucas. Jim and Elisabeth's year-old daughter played with the children of his killers.

All six of those killers would eventually give their lives to Christ. Said one of them, "Jesus' blood has washed my heart clean. My heart is healed." The Good News of Jesus Christ has since spread through the Auca Indians.

Before he went into the jungle, Jim Elliot told his wife, "If that's the way God wants it to be, I'm ready to die for the salvation of the Aucas." He was totally committed to God; Christ's willingness to lay down His life for others lived in Jim Elliot. The ripples from Jim Elliot's death are still moving across the world— because Jim Elliot's life helps us to see Christ a little more clearly.

RECOMMENDED READING: *Through Gates of Splendor* by Elisabeth Elliot (Harper & Row)

BILLY GRAHAM
A MAN OF INTEGRITY

We don't go around preaching about ourselves;
we preach Christ Jesus, the Lord.
2 CORINTHIANS 4:5

Like all the men and women in this book, Billy Graham has focused his life on Jesus Christ. Today few people who live their lives under the media's constant scrutiny can escape the shadow of scandal and disgrace, but Billy's reputation remains clean and untarnished. As the years go by, Billy seems only to grow more and more transparent to the Spirit who lives within him.

Billy Graham was born in North Carolina in 1918, the firstborn child of strict and sturdy parents. He was an active child, to say the least, and his parents would have been surprised had they known his destiny. Says one of his biographers, "He careened through early childhood at full throttle, gleefully overturning egg baskets, knocking plates from the kitchen table, sending a bureau chest crashing down a full flight of stairs, and pelting a passing auto with rocks, all less from any obvious sense of meanness than from a simple desire to see what effect his actions would produce." To counteract his mischievous nature, his mother drummed Bible verses into him at the breakfast table and while she scrubbed his back in the bathtub. The first one he learned was John 3:16.

In 1933, when Billy was a teenager, a group of church men met in the Grahams' pasture for a daylong time of prayer and fasting. At the same time, Billy's mother hosted a daylong prayer meeting inside the house. The men and women pleaded all day with God to break through the Depression's clouds and change their town. The leader of the men eventually moved from Charlotte to the entire state of North Carolina, and from there to the world, begging God to raise up someone from Charlotte that would preach the Gospel "to the ends of the earth."

The men would have been startled if they had known that the answer to their prayers was doing his chores just a few hundred yards away. Billy would have been equally surprised. When a friend came by and asked why all the cars were parked on the property, Billy gave an offhand answer: "Oh, I guess they are just some fanatics who talked Dad into letting them use the place."

As a more immediate answer to their prayers, revival did come to Charlotte. A revivalist named Mordecai Ham breathed fire and brimstone every Sunday from late August until Thanksgiving, and the Grahams were usually in the congregation. Billy said later, "This man would stand up there and point his finger at you and name all the sins you had committed. It made you think your mother had been talking to him."

As Billy listened, he realized that even though he had gone to church all his life, even though he had memorized Bible verse after Bible verse, he had still never committed his life to Christ. "Right there," he said later, "I made my decision for Christ. It was as simple as that, and as conclusive." His life would never be the same.

Although he still did not foresee that he would one day be a preacher, preaching fascinated him even then. He went on to Wheaton College where he experienced a definite call to the ministry. There he also met his wife, Ruth.

At first Billy preached in jails and on the streets, in open-air pavilions and outside saloons. As he gained experience and skill, country churches began to invite him to speak as a supply pastor. Eventually, he pastored a small Baptist church, but Billy was not skilled as a pastor. God had given him other gifts, gifts that would flourish when he found his place in worldwide evangelism.

More than any other person, Billy has shaped, and continues to influence, the course of evangelical Christianity. For over forty years he has preached in person to 70 million people in more than seventy countries, and to hundreds of millions of others on radio and television. He has been the friend and spiritual adviser of world leaders and a part of presidential inaugurations, yet he has never lost his clear-eyed focus on Christ and the Bible.

For all that, Billy Graham is no faultless saint. He is as human as anyone, as his wife Ruth knows very well.

Ruth Bell had a hard time deciding to marry Billy. She had always felt called to be a missionary to China, and she knew that marrying Billy would mean giving up her call in favor of his to evangelism. Although they were both very much in love, the young Billy could be tactless and harsh. "I'll do the leading and you do the following," he told her firmly. With difficulty, because she loved him and because she loved God, Ruth surrendered her vocation to the mission field and married him.

On the way home from their honeymoon Ruth caught a chill, just before Billy was scheduled to preach in Ohio. Instead of canceling and staying with his new wife, Billy checked her into the hospital and sent her a telegram and a box of candy. Ruth could not help but be hurt, but she soon learned that in Billy's life nothing came before preaching.

Marriage to Billy required many adjustments on Ruth's part. She had a quick tongue, an assertive temper, and she was used to a family where men listened and respected the advice of women. Billy, on the other hand, told her bluntly, "I have never taken your advice, and I don't intend to begin now."

Ruth's response was quick. "I'd be ashamed to admit that I had married a woman whose advice I didn't respect."

Another time Billy and some of his bachelor friends decided to go to Chicago. When Ruth eagerly ran to get her coat to go with them, Billy told her firmly, "No, we guys just want to be alone. No women today." As Ruth watched him drive away, through her tears she prayed, "God, if You'll forgive me for marrying him, I'll never do it again."

Over the years, though, Ruth has tempered Billy's insensitivity, just as the Spirit of Christ has continued to work on him, refining his fiery harshness into a loving spirit of humility. Patricia Cornwall, Ruth's biographer, describes Billy as a "humble, unaffected human being."

She says, "He walks into a room in jeans, his shirt half tucked in, telling Ruth he can't find his glasses (because he has them on). He acts as if I'm doing him a favor whenever I spend time with them. He's always seemed to think that other people are more famous than he is."

Maurice Wood, Bishop of Norwich and a member of the British House of Lords, says this of Billy: "I believe that in each generation God raises up certain people He can trust with success. I would put Billy in line with the Wesleys and St. Augustine. . . . And what's extraordinary is that he doesn't seem to know it. He doesn't want a Graham church. . . . He wants to be a servant of the Church, to challenge and spark the churches to be what they must become: the evangelizing agents of God and His Word. But there's no doubt about it; he is the most spiritually productive servant of God in our time."

Like John Bunyan so many years before him, Billy Graham does not ever seem to feel that he has "arrived" at the holiness God wants for him. Instead, he continues to grow in grace, as his commitment to Jesus never wavers. Billy says of himself: "I am an evangelist. But I am a man who is still in process."

RECOMMENDED READING: *Just as I Am* by Billy Graham (Harper Collins)

BROTHER LAWRENCE
A LIFE LIVED IN GOD'S PRESENCE

You will show me the way of life,
granting me the joy of your presence.
PSALM 16:11

W e shouldn't get tired of doing little things for the love of God. God looks not on the size of the job, but on the love with which we do it. We shouldn't be surprised, though, if in the beginning we often failed when we tried to live our life this way—but in the end we will form new habits that will allow us to live this way effortlessly and joyfully." When we are discouraged with ourselves or when we think we have little to offer to God's kingdom, we would do well to listen to these words of advice, written more than 300 years ago. After all, Brother Lawrence added, "The greater perfection a soul longs for, the more dependent it is on God's grace."

In 1614 Nicholas Herman (Brother Lawrence) was born in Lorraine, France. His parents were devout Catholics who taught their son to love God and the Church. At the age of eighteen, however, Nicholas's simple life was interrupted when he became a soldier in the Thirty Years' War. He conducted his military service satisfactorily, but when he returned home, he continued to be haunted by memories of the savage fighting and atrocities. Consumed with guilt and anguish, one winter day he found himself staring at a bare tree that was stripped of all its leaves.

God used this ordinary tree to speak to Nicholas's heart. The young veteran must have felt as barren and naked as the tree, his spiritual life stripped down to the bare bones. Yet, he suddenly realized, like the tree he too would grow leaves again; his life would bloom and give way to fruit. Years later, someone who knew him was to write, "It was then that he received an insight into the providence and power of God, which in the time since then has never been erased from his soul."

Shortly afterward he met a man who had renounced all his wealth to become a hermit, and for a time Nicholas tried this way of life as a means of dedicating himself to Christ's service. The hermit's solitary existence only sank him deeper into confusion and despair, however, and he decided that he needed to be surrounded by a religious congregation that would provide his fragmented spiritual life with structure and order. When he was twenty-six, he went to Paris and applied for admission at a Carmelite monastery. The Carmelites accepted him and gave him the name Brother Lawrence of the Resurrection.

His superiors assigned him to the monastery kitchen, and there he was to spend much of his life. Although he did the most menial tasks without complaint, committing himself to living in God's presence, for ten years his spiritual life was one of anguish and discouragement. Eventually, though, he reached the point where he found himself experiencing God's presence constantly in his life.

The secret, he had learned, was to let nothing come between him and God, not even his own failures. When his spiritual eyes lost their focus, he simply turned them back to God, keeping them fixed on Him not only while worshipping in prayer and song, but also in the midst of life's ordinary duties. "Busy times," he said, "are no different for me than prayer times. In my kitchen's noise and clatter, while several people are all calling for different things, I possess God just as peacefully as if I were on my knees at the altar, ready to take communion."

Later, when crippling gout made him unable to continue his kitchen duties, he was transferred to the monastery's shoe repair shop. He continued without complaint, rejoicing always in God's continual presence in his life. "God," he wrote to a friend, "has infinite treasures to give us—and yet we limit ourselves to brief, sensible prayers. Blind as we are, we get in God's way and block the flow of His grace. But when He finds a heart filled with living faith, He pours His grace into it abundantly. It flows there the way a torrent that has been blocked from its regular course will pour through whatever opening it can find, an overwhelming and abundant flood." Brother Lawrence's heart was wide open to God—and grace streamed into him, filling him full.

Brother Lawrence wrote very little, and he destroyed much of what he did write because he thought it to be worthless. After his death, his superior put together some of Brother Lawrence's letters and wrote down what he could remember of his own conversations with Brother Lawrence. Together these form a slim little book that has influenced generations of Christians: *The Practice of the Presence of God.*

Brother Lawrence died in the monastery in 1691. He had been a clumsy, unattractive man who had done only the most humble and ordinary work. He went to no mission field, he accomplished no great deeds, and he lacked any particular genius or talent. Unlike other people of faith in this book, he never broke away from the established church of his day but rather lived humbly and quietly in submission to the authority of his monastery. And yet because he was completely surrendered to God, with his entire life focused on God's presence, God's Spirit filled him and used him. His thoughts continue even today to point the way toward the practice of the presence of God.

RECOMMENDED READING: *The Practice of the Presence of God,* by Brother Lawrence, updated in today's language by Ellyn Sanna (Barbour Publishing, Inc.)

C. S. LEWIS
A MAN PURSUED BY JOY

You will be filled with my joy.
Yes, your joy will overflow!
JOHN 15:11

In the lives described in this book we see that God used many means to bring men and women to the place where He could use them for His kingdom. With some He used the vehicles we take for granted, such as church services and Christian parents and the witness of other Christians. With others He used dreams, overheard chance conversations, and nature. With C. S. Lewis, God used an illusive quality that Lewis called "Joy" to point the way to Himself.

C. S. Lewis was born in Dublin in 1898 to a solicitor and a clergyman's daughter. His mother died when he was a boy, taking with her all the dependable sources of "Joy" that he had known until then. In his own words, "With my mother's death all settled happiness, all that was tranquil and reliable, disappeared from my life. There was to be much fun, many pleasures, many stabs of Joy; but no more of the old security. It was sea and islands [of Joy] now; the great continent [of Joy] had sunk like Atlantis."

The life C. S. Lewis embarked on after his mother's death was a very intellectual one. A clumsy boy who hated sports, he found most of his pleasures in books and academics, the worlds of thought and imagination. Coming from a home life that was dry and unemotional (he was close to his older brother, but not to his father), it was little wonder that Lewis grew up to be a Cambridge professor, gifted in words and logic. He was also an atheist.

But that illusive Joy continued to pursue him. Sometimes it took him by surprise in tales of magic and fantasy; other times it overtook him while he was enjoying nature; again and again he found it in the mythology of the ancient Norse and Celts. And then he found it, stronger than ever before, in an adult fairy tale called *Phantastes* by a nineteenth-century Christian writer named George MacDonald. From then on something inside C. S. Lewis changed. Being the sort of person he was, he needed years more before his intellect would catch up with what his imagination had already grasped.

Church had little appeal for C. S. Lewis. (In fact, although he would one day become Christianity's greatest apologist, respected and loved by the entire church in all its many forms, as a mature Christian he confessed that church attendance for him was a statement of faith, rather than an experience that fed his soul.) But God wanted C. S. Lewis to be His own, and He continued to pursue him, using the voices that He knew Lewis would hear, the voices found in books. After MacDonald, Lewis next stumbled across the writings of G. K. Chesterton.

Said Lewis, "In reading Chesterton, as in reading MacDonald, I did not know what I was letting myself in for. A young man who wishes to remain a sound Atheist cannot be too careful of his reading. There are traps everywhere. . . . God is, if I may say it, very unscrupulous." Even the other academics that Lewis met at Cambridge spoke to him of Christianity. He began to feel as though he were in a chess game with God, fighting with all the powers of his considerable intellect, yet being put in check at every turn. Soon, he would no longer be able to avoid checkmate.

"I felt as if I were a man of snow at long last beginning to melt," he wrote later. "The melting was starting in my back—drip-drip and presently trickle-trickle. I rather disliked the feeling. . . . People who are naturally religious find difficulty in understanding the horror. . . . Amiable agnostics will talk cheerfully about 'man's search for God.' To me, as I then was, they might as well have talked about the mouse's search for the cat.

"You must picture me alone. . .night after night, feeling, whenever my mind lifted even for a second from my work, the steady, unrelenting approach of Him whom I so desired not to meet. That which I greatly feared had at last come upon me. . . . I gave in, and admitted that God was God, and knelt and prayed: perhaps, that night, the most dejected and reluctant convert in all England. I did not then see what is now the most shining and obvious thing; the Divine humility which will accept a convert even on such terms."

Once C. S. Lewis opened himself to God, he never turned back. From then on his powerful intellect became God's tool, and his gift for words was used to spread the Good News through his nonfiction, novels, and children's stories. Without God, he would still have been a brilliant thinker and writer, but the world would not have been changed by his works on medieval literature the way it was by his thoughts on Christianity. He had a gift for writing in a way that could be understood by ordinary people, and yet his books also made the intellectual and academic world take Christianity seriously.

Despite his fame and success, his life was a quiet one, and not always easy. He fell in love and married late in his life, only to have his wife (whose name was Joy) die of cancer after a few short years. Since his conversion, his faith had always been solid and unshakable, built firmly on logic and rational thinking, but grief knocked away all the well-thought-out answers he had depended on so long. Shaken and blind with grief, his faith seemed to have deserted him—but God had not. The same God who left a trail of Joy through his whole life for him to follow, the same God who had pursued him so relentlessly, did not abandon him. The faith that he describes in *A Grief Observed* is humbler than the one he outlines so vigorously in *Mere Christianity,* but it also rings truer. Perhaps God allowed Lewis to experience pain and heartache so that he (and we) could see that even when we seem to lose the things on which we have depended all our lives, God does not fail.

C. S. Lewis died quietly at the age of sixty-five while reading in his garden. His death was barely noticed by the world since John F. Kennedy was assassinated on the same day. Years earlier, in one of his *Narnia* tales, Lewis had written of that moment when life ends:

"For them it was only the beginning of the real story. All their life in this world. . .had only been the cover and title page: now at last they were beginning Chapter One of the Great Story, which no one on earth has read: which goes on for ever: in which every chapter is better than the one before."

There, in that moment, at the beginning of a new eternal story, C.S. Lewis surely found Joy.

RECOMMENDED READING: *Surprised by Joy: The Shape of My Early Life* by C. S. Lewis (Harcourt, Brace & World)

ERIC LIDDELL
THE MAN WHO RODE CHARIOTS OF FIRE

Suddenly a chariot of fire appeared,
drawn by horses of fire.
It drove between them, separating them,
and Elijah was carried by
a whirlwind into heaven.
2 KINGS 2:11

The 1982 movie *Chariots of Fire,* which won an Academy Award for Best Picture, told the story of the rivalry between two legendary runners, Harold Abrahams of England and Eric Liddell of Scotland. But deeper than that engaging tale, the film called viewers to examine the importance of faith in one's life, and the lengths to which one man would go to be true to his Christian commitment.

As the movie tells, Eric Liddell's Christian convictions kept him from running the 100-meter race at the 1924 Olympics in Paris. The qualifying heats for the race were held on a Sunday, and as a result, Eric made a decision that was viewed as tantamount to treason by the world's standards: He gave up his chance for an Olympic medal because of his belief that he was not to participate in such an activity on God's day. Instead, Liddell was allowed to compete in the 400-meter race, an event that he had little or no likelihood of winning. He was further handicapped when he drew an outside lane where no other runners would help him set his pace. Despite the odds, he raced to victory, winning by five meters, and returned to Scotland a hero.

That is where the movie ends, but it is only the beginning of Eric's story. The year after his Olympic victory, he chose to turn his back on fame and commit the rest of his life to serving Jesus Christ. Following in his parents' footsteps, Eric became a missionary to China, where he assumed a teaching position at the Anglo-Chinese Christian College in Tientsin.

In his spare time, Eric did continue to run, but running for sport made no sense to the Chinese. They looked at him oddly when he dashed through the crowded streets, dodging vendors and pedestrians, and so he stopped his daily running routine. God had more important business for him.

When the Japanese invaded China, Eric chose to stay, knowing the danger. He could have joined his wife and children, who were safely transported to Canada, but he knew his place was with the struggling Chinese people. He was soon rounded up with other foreign missionaries and business people and spent the rest of his life in an internment camp, enduring bitter conditions and the ever-present threat of death. He died of a brain tumor just a few months before liberation in 1945. God had separated Eric from those around him, just as He had the prophet Elijah, and in the midst of earthly confusion and tumult, carried Eric into His presence.

One of his fellow prisoners wrote these words about Eric: "He unreservedly committed his life to Jesus Christ as his Savior and Lord. That friendship meant everything to him. By the flickering light of a peanut-oil lamp early each morning, he studied the Bible and talked with God for an hour every day. As a Christian Eric Liddell's desire was to know God more deeply; and as a missionary to make Him known more fully."

This is the sort of dedication that earns a place in God's hall of fame. "None of us," his fellow prisoner wrote, "will ever forget this man who was totally committed to putting God first, a man whose humble life combined muscular Christianity with radiant godliness."

RECOMMENDED READING: *Eric Liddell* by Catherine Swift (Bethany House Publishers)

MARTIN LUTHER
THE MAN WHO PREACHED CHRIST

Salvation is not a reward for
the good things we have done.
EPHESIANS 2:9

Some people who are called by God have conversion experiences like Saul of Tarsus: A burst of blinding light changes their identities forever. In her own quiet way, this was the sort of conversion that Fanny Crosby experienced at that revival altar. Others, however, like John Bunyan, Brother Lawrence, and Martin Luther found conversion a slow and painful process, spending years agonizing over doubts and insecurities.

Martin Luther was born in 1483 in Saxony. Both his parents were deeply spiritual people, hardworking, upright, and used to making up their own minds. They passed these values along to their son, while providing him with a first-class education, first at a boys' school and then at one of Germany's most prestigious universities.

From his childhood, Luther was deeply interested in religion, but these feelings were intensified at the end of his university years when he had a terrifying brush with death. He realized then that he was not ready to make the journey through death, and he vowed to become a monk, hoping to fit himself to face God. At the age of twenty-two he entered the monastery.

The discipline of holy orders brought him no peace; rather, his anxieties became sharper and more obsessive. He could never feel certain that he had confessed all his sins or done all that he needed to do to achieve holiness. Eventually, he realized he was trying to climb a "ladder to heaven," something constructed by human intellect or effort. His efforts were as hopeless as trying to pull himself up by his own bootstraps; any ladder he constructed was destined to collapse under his first steps, sending him plummeting away from God.

At last, when he was twenty-five, he was called to serve at the University of Wittenberg. There his vicar-general, a deeply spiritual man who was firmly grounded in the Bible, helped Luther come to terms with his pain and uncertainty. The vicar-general advised Luther to turn away from his obsessive doubts and instead focus on seeking peace with God. He could do this, said the vicar-general, not through his own strength and resolution, or through good works, but simply because of God's grace and mercy. In other words, like Brother Lawrence and John Bunyan before him, Luther had to stop looking at himself and his own failures and achievements and instead look only at Christ. God sent Christ, said the vicar-general, not as a condemning judge to point out all our flaws and inadequacy, but as a Savior who will make us whole.

Luther, however, continued to be troubled. Lashed by his conscience and his heavy load of sin, he went to Rome to climb the Sancta Scala, or the "holy stairs." People believed that if one climbed what were said to be the same stairs Christ climbed at the beginning of the Via Dolorosa, on hands and knees and praying on each step, God would grant absolution for sins. Luther decided to give it a try, hoping finally to be rid of his heavy burden of guilt.

As he started up the stairs, repeating a prayer on each step, halfway through his journey a voice seemed to speak in his soul: *The just shall live by faith.* At last, Luther's spiritual and mental shackles dropped away. In his own words, he realized that "His mercy is my justification. . . . The gates of paradise had been flung open and I had entered. There and then the whole of Scripture took on another look to me."

Luther went back to Germany, and from that time on he used his position at the university as a pulpit from which to preach his new revelation. His goal was to reform the Catholic church by turning the church's focus away from works and back to Christ's grace. He never sought to start a new church, but his enthusiasm and fire lit the Protestant Reformation that swept through Europe. His only concern, however, had been to preach Christ; this was the mission God had given him, and to Luther no other achievement mattered.

When Luther died at the age of sixty-three, he was no longer troubled by fear and doubts. Although the beginning of his spiritual journey had been cloudy and painful, he had kept going, step by step through the darkness of sin and selfishness, until at last he came out into the light of grace.

"My soul stays with Christ," he wrote. "With these words I shall go to bed in the evening and arise in the morning; on them I shall rely, on them I shall sleep, wake, and work, and with them cross the final bridge of death into eternal life.

"Seek yourself only in Christ and not in yourself; and then you will find yourself in Him eternally."

RECOMMENDED READING: *Here I Stand* by Roland Bainton (Templegate)

DWIGHT L. MOODY
GOD'S EVANGELIST

The believers. . .went everywhere
preaching the Good News about Jesus.
ACTS 8:4

Dwight Moody (1837–1899) was the Billy Graham of the nineteenth century—albeit an unordained man with no formal training—who went on to found a church, three schools, summer conference centers, and a publishing agency. A riveting speaker, he touched hundreds of thousands, if not millions of people, all in the days before radio or television. His life shows how God can use an ordinary person to extend His kingdom, when that person is open and dedicated to God.

As a young man Dwight Moody was not sure what road he should travel down. Lacking purpose and direction, his youth showed little promise of the life that God had in store for him. To support himself, he went to Boston to look for work. At last, homesick and discouraged, he went to his uncles and asked if they would give him work in their shoe store. They agreed, provided he would promise to attend church and Sunday school and not drink or gamble.

Moody became the store's errand boy and eventually worked his way up to being a salesman. He kept his promise and attended church, but his life continued to be dictated by selfishness and an unruly temper. His Sunday school teacher, a man named Mr. Kimball, felt led to make a special effort to speak to Moody alone about his salvation.

As Mr. Kimball later told Moody's son Will, "I was determined to speak to him about Christ and his soul and started down to Holton's shoe store. When I was nearly there, I began to wonder whether I ought to go in just then during business hours. I thought that possibly my call might embarrass the boy and then when I went away the other clerks would ask who I was and taunt him with my efforts. In the meantime I had passed the store and, discovering this, I determined to make a dash for it and have it over at once. I found Moody in the back part of the building wrapping up shoes. I went up to him at once, and, putting my hands on his shoulders, I made what I afterwards felt was a very weak plea for Christ. I simply told him of Christ's love for him and the love Christ wanted in return. That was all there was. It seemed the young man was just ready for the light that then broke upon him, and there, in the back of that store in Boston, he gave himself and his life to Christ."

The apostle Paul found Christ while on the road to Damascus, when a bright light blinded him and transformed his life forever. Dwight Moody saw the same transforming light in the back of a shoe store.

"Before my conversion," Moody said later, "I worked toward the Cross, but since then I have worked from the Cross; then I worked to be saved, now I work because I am saved."

RECOMMENDED READING: *D. L. Moody* by William Moody (Moody Press)

SAMUEL MORRIS
THE MAN WHO HEARD THE HOLY GHOST

*All these faithful ones died without receiving
what God had promised them,
but they saw it all from a distance
and welcomed the promises of God.*
HEBREWS 11:13

As westerners, we tend to restrict God's behavior
to the actions that make sense to minds steeped in the
scientific tradition. We are usually uncomfortable with
a faith that claims to touch God in ways that seem too
extreme or supernatural. God works in many ways, however, and He uses whatever material is at hand. Sometimes He works quietly and circumspectly through the
books we read, the churches we attend, and the influence of our parents and friends. In the life of Samuel
Morris, though, God spoke directly and dramatically.

A hundred years ago Prince Kaboo was born in the
forests of Liberia. His father was the chief of the Kru
people, and Kaboo grew up surrounded by love and
attention. When he was an adolescent, though, his people were attacked by their enemies, the Grebos, and
Kaboo was taken captive.

The Grebos took him in place of the rest of his
people, just as Christ was once sacrificed in the place
of humanity. The Grebos tortured Kaboo and tied him
to a cross-tree made from two logs. Kaboo expected
to die there.

Instead, he heard a loud voice saying, "Get up,
Kaboo. Get up and run!" A bright light flashed around

him, but before Kaboo could see who was speaking to him, the ropes fell from him. His enemies appeared stunned, their eyes blinded, as Kaboo ran away, deep into the jungle.

The light continued to lead him, showing him the path to take, pointing out fruits and nuts and roots that he could eat. Eventually, the light led him to a plantation. There he met people who had once been slaves in America but were now free. They told Kaboo of a God who had sent His son to die for His people. This Son had hung on a cross-tree, just as Kaboo had. Kaboo also learned of a man named Paul who had seen a great, blinding light and heard a voice speaking from heaven. Kaboo knew then who had rescued him from his enemies.

Kaboo gave his life to Jesus Christ. To symbolize his new identity now that he belonged to God, he changed his name to Samuel Morris.

Prince Kaboo had grown up with a people who talked to their ancestors' ghosts, asking them for help and protection. Now, Sammy began to talk to the Holy Ghost. He talked to Him every day, every hour, and he listened for the Holy Ghost's answers. The Holy Ghost told him to take a boat to America, where Sammy would learn more about God.

When Sammy finally reached America, people thought he was an ugly black man dressed in rags. They rejected him and refused to listen to his message. Sammy, however, kept right on talking with the Holy Ghost.

Although he could barely read or write, he went to

Taylor University. His goal was to learn more about God so that he could go back to his own people and teach them. He studied hard and gradually he earned the university's acceptance and support. His openness and lack of sophistication won people's hearts, and his faith challenged them to change their lives. In the end, his influence changed Taylor's entire nature. Wherever he went and with whomever he spoke the joy and love that lived in him radiated outward.

Physically, however, Sammy was having a hard time adjusting to the cold climate. The first snow that he saw filled him with awe; each snowflake, he said, was a "message from heaven." But his ears ached so badly that he cried, begging God to help him. The pain in his ears went away, he said, because the Holy Ghost blew on them, making them warm.

The next winter, though, Sammy became even sicklier. From the hospital he pleaded with God to make him better again, but this time his requests were denied. Puzzled that the Holy Ghost had not responded as He always had before, Sammy then saw the same light that he had seen years earlier in the jungles of Africa. Inside the light were angels coming to take him home. Sammy knew then that his work was finished.

"But you can't go," his friends told him. "We need you here. What about your work back in Africa? What about the children there who are waiting for you to teach them?"

Sammy just smiled. "It's not my work," he told them. "It's God's. He will choose who He wants to go to the children in Africa. I've finished my job on earth. It's

time to go home." His smile grew wider. "I'm so glad."
Still smiling, Sammy went home.

The short life of Samuel Morris acted as a cata-
lyst, bringing ripples of change to all who had known
him. Taylor University was swept with revival, and as
Sammy knew, God led many missionaries to Africa.
Sammy's "children" would learn very soon about the
God—and Holy Ghost—who loved them.

RECOMMENDED READING: *Samuel Morris* by W. Terry
Whalin (Barbour Publishing, Inc.)

MOTHER TERESA
MISSIONARY OF CHARITY

"I assure you,
when you did it to one of the least
of these my brothers and sisters,
you were doing it to me!"
MATTHEW 25:40

Let us put ourselves completely under the power and influence of Jesus, so that He may think with our minds, work with our hands, for we can do all things if His strength is with us." So said Mother Teresa, who, like the others in this book, lived a life that was totally focused on Jesus Christ. In her case, this focus expressed itself in an overwhelming concern for the world's poor. In the poor she saw Jesus, and by caring for them, she showed her love for her Lord.

Agnes Gonxha Bojaxhiu was born in 1910 in Yugoslavia, the daughter of an Albanian chemist. She grew up learning about God, and at the age of twelve she decided to consecrate her life totally to Him. When she was eighteen she entered a religious order that sent her to Calcutta, India. There she took the name Sister Teresa.

For the next ten years she worked in a school connected to the convent, but all the while the desperate poverty in the streets of Calcutta haunted her. The Holy Spirit was calling to her through the poor, asking her to give herself even more deeply to Christ. But what could she do? She was a slight woman and her health was threatened by tuberculosis. And yet again and again, she heard a voice calling her, insisting that she must do something.

In the summer of 1946 Sister Teresa went by train to Darjeeling to make her annual retreat. All the way there she was obsessed with images she had seen in Calcutta's streets: stinking slums, dying children, dogs eating living fetuses, a little boy whose mother had tried to strangle him. Although she had left Calcutta behind, she could not escape the horrifying memories of desperate poverty and degradation. At last she surrendered to God's call: She would leave her order and devote herself entirely to the poor.

Although she faced opposition from her superiors, eventually she received permission to leave the convent. After taking a three-month course from an order of medical sisters, she sought out Calcutta's most miserable slums. She went from one hut to the next, washing and feeding all the children she could find. After three days she started an open-air school, welcoming twenty-three pupils on the first day, forty-one the second. She began each school day by washing all her students. Lessons were learned by writing on the dusty ground, Sister Teresa's "blackboard."

As she lived and worked with the poorest of the poor, she often remembered the comfortable life she had led within the convent. In the face of her temptation, she prayed resolutely, "My God, because of my free choice and for love of You alone, I am going to stay here and do what Your will demands of me." She began to look for those homeless people who were too weak to move, their bodies stretched out on the pavements, lying so still she could barely tell the dead from the living. The first woman she took off the street was half-eaten by rats and ants; another old woman had been thrown out with the garbage by her son. Teresa took them to the hospital and insisted that they be given medical care.

Each day, as she worked all alone until she was exhausted, the temptation to return to her order grew stronger and stronger. Still, she insisted to herself, "The Lord wants me exactly where I am—He will provide the answers." Just when she thought she could hold out no longer, the Lord did provide. A government official gave her a room to use, and help and support began to pour in from teachers, students, and mothers of families. Teresa was no longer alone.

Eventually, in 1950, Mother Teresa founded a new order, the Missionary Sisters of Charity. To care for the poor and homeless and the sick and dying, the now international order began Homes for the Dying, as well as orphanages, maternity homes, and schools.

In 1997 Mother Teresa died at the age of eighty-seven. Up until the time of her death, despite ill health and frequent hospitalizations, she worked for Christ and His kingdom with a tireless energy. And her order continues to work for Christ, albeit without her dynamic vision and leadership. Her successor, Sister Narmala, admits, "This is an awesome responsibility, but I am trusting in God and His grace for the present, moment by moment."

Once Mother Teresa was asked by a starving beggar woman why she was washing the festering sores that covered her body. Mother Teresa responded, "For the love of Christ." That love for Christ—and not the rewards and awards the world had to to offer—was the one thing that shaped Mother Teresa's entire life, molding it into an instrument God could use to touch our world. That same love can shape our lives also.

As Mother Teresa said, "Let us be open to God so that He can use us. Let us put our love into actions, beginning in the family, in the neighborhood, in the street. It is difficult, but there is where the work begins. We are coworkers of Christ, a fruitbearing branch of the vine."

RECOMMENDED READING: *Something Beautiful for God* by Malcolm Muggeridge and *The Love of Christ: Spiritual Counsels* by Mother Teresa of Calcutta (both from Harper & Row)

WATCHMAN NEE
GOD'S PRISONER

Hear my cry, for I am very low.
Rescue me from my persecutors,
for they are too strong for me.
Bring me out of prison so I can thank you.
PSALM 142:6–7

Few of us are called to serve God in an actual prison, but many of us are imprisoned by the circumstances of our lives. When we feel trapped, we are apt to make excuses for ourselves; after all, how can God expect our best from us when we are suffering such hardship? God's grace shines at its most brilliant, however, in the lives of those who have experienced actual imprisonment, men like John Bunyan and Watchman Nee. Nee's life challenges us to find God even in darkness and suffering.

Henry Nee was born in China in 1903 to Christian parents. When Henry was seventeen his mother's rededication of her life to Christ deeply touched him, and, as a result, he went to hear evangelist Dora Yu. Years later, he described his feelings at that meeting:

"For the first time in my life, I saw myself as a sinner, and I also saw the Savior. I saw the Lord's hands nailed to the Cross, stretching forth His arms to welcome me, saying, 'I am here waiting to receive you.' Overwhelmed by such love, I could not possibly reject it."

After that Henry was never the same. As is customary in Chinese culture, he chose a new name to symbolize the turning point in his life: To-sheng, or Watchman. Like the prophets of the Old Testament, Watchman felt called to act as spiritual guard for his nation, warning his country of God's judgment even as he reminded them of His great love.

Once Watchman Nee came to Christ, he began to pore over the Bible and the writings of spiritual men like John Bunyan. An English missionary named Margaret Barber provided him with more spiritual training, setting him on the path he would follow for the rest of his life. She inspired him with her radical devotion to the cross of Christ and her fiery passion for His Word.

"Stay broken," she told him often. "Don't listen to the compliments people give you. You must stay broken. Christ is most pleased with brokenness. Remember the cross."

Miss Barber made sure Watchman learned this lesson, as well as many others. Like Amy Carmichael, Miss Barber found no basis in the Bible for denominationalism. She knew that Christ's body must be one, not separated by differences in practice or vocabulary. She also taught Watchman that he could live by faith, trusting God to meet each need as it arose, just as Hudson Taylor had in his ministry.

Although he encountered opposition from the traditional denominations, Watchman Nee set to work establishing indigenous churches in China. His ministry flourished as he continued to live totally focused on the Gospel of Christ, and the books he wrote during this time reflect that wholehearted devotion.

When he was imprisoned in 1952 by the Chinese

government for the crime of being Christian, he began to touch more lives for Christ than ever before. An almost legendary figure, Watchman Nee caught the attention of the world and his books became international best-sellers. In the end, he became a symbol of what Christianity really means, and his life called western Christians to a deeper and more radical faith.

In 1972, after twenty years of imprisonment and torture, Watchman Nee died in the Shanghai prison. Shortly before his death, he wrote to his sister, "I maintain my own joy." This joy that never failed him, despite his circumstances, sprang from Christ and His Spirit.

"Nothing hurts so much," he once said, "as dissatisfaction with our circumstances. We all start from rest, but there is another rest which we discover when we learn from Jesus how to say, 'I thank You, Father, for it seemed good to Thee.' God knows what He is doing and there is nothing accidental in the life of the believer. Nothing but good can come to those who are wholly His."

RECOMMENDED READING: *Changed Into His Likeness* (Christian Literature Crusade) and *Living Sacrifice* (Christian Fellowship Publishing) by Watchman Nee

JOHN NEWTON
A SLAVE TRADER SAVED BY GRACE

God can always point to us as examples
of the incredible wealth of his favor
and kindness toward us,
as shown in all he has done for us
through Christ Jesus.
EPHESIANS 2:7

John Newton was one of those children who seem to fall through the cracks, children who grow up without enough love or safety, only to turn into damaged men and women who live wasted, violent lives, perhaps hurting yet another generation of children. As Christians, we should do all we can to help stop this dark cycle— but we should also remember that God is not limited by the human influences in a person's life. As John Newton's life proves, even God's nature can bear the message of grace.

In England, in 1725, John Newton was born to a Christian mother. Although she died when John was only six, she had managed to speak to her son about God's grace. Apparently, a seed was planted that was to lie dormant until John was an adult.

After her death John's home life became unbearable. When he was eleven he ran away from home and became a sailor, and his life went steadily downhill from there. Finding the existence of a sailor nearly as cruel as his home life, he ran away again, only to be captured by a press-gang. Later he deserted the Royal Navy but was recaptured, publicly flogged as a criminal, and eventually abandoned in Africa. For a time he was imprisoned as a slave to a Portuguese slave trader, only to escape and join a slave ship. Newton would later describe these years of his life as "sad and wanton profligacy." When he gave any thought to Christianity, he did so with hatred and bitterness.

After years spent in such dissolution, a storm at sea brought a miraculous change to John Newton. When the heavy winds that had threatened to capsize his ship at last subsided, the vessel was battered and limping, with no provisions or sails. Somehow, though, the shipmates survived cold and starvation and finally made their way to Ireland.

Of this time, John Newton said later, "I began to know there is a God that hears and answers prayers." Although he had miraculously escaped death before, somehow God spoke clearly to him through this particular storm. Said Newton, "The Lord had wrought a marvelous thing: I was sincerely touched with a sense of the undeserved mercy I had received. Thus to all appearance, I was a new man." The seed his mother had planted so many years before had at last germinated.

A new person, Newton began to work resolutely for the kingdom of God. He wrote eloquently and vigorously against the slave trade, inspiring William Wilberforce, who would become the great British emancipator. Among the more than 280 hymns he wrote, lyrics that are still sung today, is his poignant gem, "Amazing Grace."

John Newton wrote this epitaph to be inscribed on his tombstone: "John Newton, Clerk, once an infidel and libertine, a servant of slaves in Africa, was, by the rich mercy of our Lord and Saviour, Jesus Christ, preserved, restored, pardoned, and appointed to preach the faith he had long laboured to destroy." He died in 1807.

That God had loved John Newton enough to continue pursuing him down through the years, until at last He found him, is reflected in this song from the heart of a former slave trader:

> *Amazing grace how sweet the sound,*
> *That saved a wretch like me!*
> *I once was lost, but now am found,*
> *Was blind but now I see.*

RECOMMENDED READING: *John Newton* by Anne Sandberg (Barbour Publishing, Inc.)

OLGA ROBERTSON
"MOMMY" TO 9,000 INMATES

Don't forget about those in prison.
Suffer with them as though
you were there yourself.
HEBREWS 13:3

When a woman's life is focused on Christ, God uses her powerfully for His kingdom, despite her chronological age. Like Mother Teresa and Corrie ten Boom, Olga Robertson was not content to spend her old age in a rocking chair. Instead, she continues to use her strength and energy to share God's love in the dark, needy world of Bilibid Prison.

Olga Robertson (born in 1923) is a Lebanese American whom God has called to the Philippines. For almost twenty years, she has worked as a spiritual counselor in the Bilibid Prison outside Manila. Far from powerful in stature, she moves freely and confidently in one of the world's largest prisons among the most hardened convicts who have embraced gangs as a way of life. But Olga offers each of them a love that is just as tough as any inmate.

She admits that she is often afraid as she works within the prison—but nothing about her conveys that fear. Instead, her laughing eyes and quick step speak of love and light to the men who await her visits so eagerly.

Through her, God's love is transforming the lives of men who have committed the worst crimes. Their nickname for her is "Mommy Olga," and in her presence murderers, rapists, and thieves turn into laughing men who can testify of the change Jesus Christ has worked in their lives.

Olga demonstrates to the unlovable that in God's eyes they are precious. She shows them that they can never be separated from Christ's love, even in prison. God's love is strong enough to go all the way to the electric chair—and Olga Robertson is strong enough to go there too. When prisoners must pay society's ultimate price for their crimes, Olga keeps them company to the end. Her life shines with Christ's enduring brilliance, a light that no darkness can extinguish.

As Olga grows older, she still has too much to do for her to slow down. Some of what she does is little, like handing out aftershave lotion to inmates, and some is not so little, like supervising a new chapel for prison guards. Big or little, each of her actions demonstrates the value Christ places on each individual, no matter what sins he may have committed.

When asked why she does what she does, this is Olga's response: "God loves them, and so do I."

RECOMMENDED READING: *Heroes: People Who Made a Difference in Our World* by Harold Sala (Promise Press)

MARY SLESSOR
QUEEN OF THE CALABAR

My Father who lives in me
does his work through me.
JOHN 14:10

Whether we are rich and sophisticated or talented and well-educated makes little difference. What matters is that we are completely surrendered to God, with our hearts wide open to His Spirit. Mary Slessor was a woman whose family background offered her little—and yet she offered everything that she was to God.

Mary Slessor was born in 1848 to an alcoholic shoemaker and an overworked mother. During this time in Scotland—known as the "Hungry Forties"—crops failed and farm workers were driven to the overburdened cities. Mary's family shared this fate, and in the slums of Dundee her father finally succumbed totally to his alcoholism. Consequently, Mary's mother labored as a weaver in a factory and at age seven Mary joined her mother at work.

Mary grew up tough, with a gritty determination and the courage to stand up for herself, qualities that would later stand her in good stead. When rowdy young men gave her a hard time, the fierce redhead was not afraid to use her fists to defend herself.

But when Mary heard a missionary from Africa speak at a local church, God reached through Mary's tough exterior and touched her heart. His call on her life seemed clear to her: She must go to Africa, to the Calabar (known now as the Sudan), to spread the Gospel.

Everyone around her doubted that call, and no one made the way easy for her to go to the mission field. Determined as always, Mary never doubted what God wanted for her life.

Years later, after she had become known as the "Queen of the Calabar," Mary wrote in her diary, "God plus one are always a majority—let me know Thou art with me." His presence in her life was all she needed to move ahead, against whatever odds confronted her.

Once she reached Africa Mary confronted even harsher opposition. Africa was a land damaged by Europeans and the wounds of the slave trade were still oozing. In the years since the end of slavery, white men had only heaped insult on injury, scarring the land, using its people, and spreading alcoholism and corruption.

Then there were the pagan customs that devalued life. When Mary learned of the native belief that all twins should be killed immediately at birth since one had been fathered by the devil, she began quietly to adopt dozens of babies. She also worked fiercely for the right of African women to protect themselves from violence and death at the hands of their husbands.

At the same time, Mary never opposed African ways if they did not hurt the Africans themselves. She was not a missionary who spread European ways, but one who spread Christ's way of love. For nearly forty years she lived among the Africans as one of them, making her home in a village hut.

After many years in Africa Mary came home to Scotland, her fiery red hair totally gray and her face wrinkled and wizened. Her friends did not recognize her, and some even feared she had taken leave of her senses. Often they heard her talking softly while all alone in her room. As it turned out, Mary was simply talking with God. She had learned to keep close to Him continually, and the habit had become automatic to her, a part of her identity.

God was truly a part of Mary. Because she so clearly loved them, the Africans came to understand God's love. Mary Slessor was God's hands and feet, and she had shown the people of the Calabar God's heart. When she died in 1915, thousands of Africans wept for Eka Kpukpro Owo, "Mother of All the People."

RECOMMENDED READING: *Mary Slessor: Queen of Calabar* by Sam Wellman (Barbour Publishing, Inc.)

CHARLES SPURGEON
A PREACHER TO SINNERS

*Your duty is to go and preach
the coming of the Kingdom of God.*
LUKE 9:60

Many of the men and women in this hall of fame have written great books or songs that have spread the Good News. Others have done great works for the poor and needy, or done nothing more spectacular than live quiet, consecrated lives. Charles Spurgeon, born in 1834, served God by preaching the Gospel to sinners.

Charles Spurgeon was the British version of the American evangelist D. L. Moody and, in fact, the two men were good friends. By the time Spurgeon was twenty-two he was the most popular preacher in England, speaking to audiences of 10,000 people. Even Queen Victoria, the titular head of the Church of England, is rumored to have gone to hear him, though dressed in disguise.

Spurgeon's influence, however, was not confined to the pulpit. Although he died in 1892, his sermons continued to be published weekly until 1917. Altogether, more than 2,000 of his sermons have been published, an enormous forty-nine-volume set of works called *The Metropolitan Pulpit.* He also founded orphanages, a Bible society, a college for clergy, and branch churches.

His message was a simple one: Trust Christ and you shall be saved. This was the Gospel, the only subject worth talking about, in Spurgeon's opinion, for this was the good news that had brought comfort to his own soul.

In his autobiography, *From the Usher's Desk to the Tabernacle Pulpit*, Spurgeon told the story of his own conversion. As a young man, he said, God had been pleased to

> *"convince me of sin. I lived a miserable creature, finding no hope, no comfort, thinking that surely God would never save me. . . . I felt I was willing to do anything and be anything if God would only forgive me. I set off. . .and went to all the places of worship; and though I dearly venerate the men, I am bound to say that I never heard them once fully preach the gospel. I mean by that, they preached truth, great truths, many good truths that were fitting to. . .their congregations, but what I wanted to know was, how can I get my sins forgiven?"*

Sometimes the simplest and most obvious thing can be the hardest to comprehend. In the midst of a snowstorm, Spurgeon once ended up in a small chapel. Since the pastor had been unable to get there because of the weather, an uneducated workingman stood up in front of the tiny congregation and spoke. He had no experience preaching, and he could barely read the text from Isaiah: "Look unto me, and be ye saved, all the ends of the earth." But he looked down at Charles Spurgeon and said, "Young man, you look very miserable."

Although Spurgeon was taken aback at being spoken to directly from the pulpit, in truth he was miserable. The man continued by saying, "You will always be miserable—miserable in life and miserable in death—if you do not obey my text. But if you obey now, this moment you will be saved." And then he leaned over the pulpit and shouted, "Young man, look to Jesus Christ!"

Charles Spurgeon did look—and like so many others in this book, his life was transformed by the light that flooded his heart. "I now think," he said afterward, "I am bound never to preach a sermon without preaching to sinners." This was the place God had for Charles Spurgeon in His kingdom.

The answer to our hearts' longings comes to us by many paths and different forms, but it is always the same answer: Jesus Christ. For Spurgeon, as with all the others in this book, the sight of Jesus was all he needed. Once he looked to Christ, he wrote, "There and then the cloud was gone, the darkness had rolled away, and that moment I saw the sun. . .the simple faith which looks alone to Him."

RECOMMENDED READING: *Charles Spurgeon* by J.C. Carlile, abridged and edited by Dan Harmon (Barbour Publishing, Inc.)

J. HUDSON TAYLOR
MISSIONARY TO CHINA

A righteous person will live by faith.
HEBREWS 10:38

The men and women in this book consecrated themselves to God, opening their hearts in absolute surrender. God used their lives to change the world in which they lived, and even the world that is ours today, through the working of the Holy Spirit. Another of God's servants, Hudson Taylor (1832–1905) left a powerful legacy that continues to influence the mission field.

Since he was a child Hudson Taylor had been drawn to China. "One day," he vowed, "I will live in China, and I will die in China." God used Taylor's fascination with China to found the China Inland Mission in the mid-nineteenth century.

On the way to China his ship was nearly shipwrecked off New Guinea. The passengers were truly caught between a rock and a hard place: If they swam to land to escape the danger of shipwreck, they would face the islanders who had already prepared huge fires on which to cook them, and if they remained at sea, they might drown or be eaten by sharks. Although their situation seemed hopeless, the ship escaped and Hudson Taylor went on his way to China.

Again and again, God worked in Taylor's life, bringing blessings out of what looked like hopeless situations. His experiences in China were full of hardship and suffering, but still he allowed God to direct his life. Taylor learned to live in complete dependence on God, and God never let him down, supplying whatever he needed in abundance. When Taylor prayed for seventy people to come help him in his work in China, seventy-eight missionaries came; whatever funds, food, or buildings were needed were also supplied with the same generous abundance. He learned to give away whatever he had, trusting God to meet his needs one day at a time. Meanwhile, God used Taylor's work to bring the Gospel to thousands of Chinese.

His was the first truly interdenominational mission, and the China Inland Mission became the pattern for world evangelization during the nineteenth century. As a "faith mission," the China Inland Mission depended more on faith in God's ability to provide than on worldly backing and funds. Taylor's approach also placed little importance on education but instead stressed the vital necessity of spiritual consecration.

Unlike many missionaries of his day, Taylor did not endorse "Christianizing"; in other words, he did not seek to change the people of other cultures into Europeans, with European customs and ways of dress. With his only aim to spread the Good News of Christ, he shocked many Europeans by dressing in Chinese fashion, right down to his long pigtail. He saw clearly that the only thing vital to Christianity is Christ Himself, and the Good News of Christ transcends cultures and customs.

Hudson Taylor died in China, just as he had wanted. Since his conversion at the age of fourteen he had surrendered himself completely to God—and in return God blessed him and his work. Taylor lived and died by the same blinding insight that had struck him when he was first converted: Christ died for our sins, and not for ours only, but for the sins of the whole world.

Once he had understood this, Taylor wrote, he wondered what there was left for him to do. "Light was flashed into my soul by the Holy Spirit, that there was nothing in the world to be done but to fall down on one's knees, and accepting the Savior and His salvation, to praise Him forevermore."

RECOMMENDED READING: *Biography of James Hudson Taylor* by Howard Taylor (Hodder & Stoughton)

CORRIE TEN BOOM
TRAMP FOR THE LORD

Though the rain comes in torrents
and the floodwaters rise
and the winds beat against that house,
it won't collapse,
because it is built on rock.
MATTHEW 7:25

As many of us reach middle age, we may feel as though the most useful and exciting part of our lives is coming to an end. Corrie ten Boom's life shows us that God does not see a person's usefulness in terms of age. Like Mother Teresa, Corrie was a tough and tireless woman, who was more visibly used in her old age than she ever was as a younger woman. From the very beginning, though, Corrie's life was built on the rock of Christ.

Corrie ten Boom was born in the Netherlands in 1892, the youngest of four children. Both her father, who was a watchmaker, and her mother were deeply spiritual people who shone with God's love. They welcomed everyone into their home, especially those who were in need. Even more unusual, her family sponsored a prayer meeting for Jews. This was the atmosphere of love and grace that nourished Corrie as a child.

Corrie became the first woman to be a licensed watchmaker in the Netherlands. Until she was fifty, she lived quietly with her father and sister, pursuing her profession, busy with her many clubs for boys and girls and the mentally retarded.

World War II destroyed the ten Booms' peaceful life. A family that had always welcomed and helped whoever was in need, they could not look away from the Jews' terrible plight. Soon they became involved in hiding and rescuing Jews, fully aware of the danger they faced if they were apprehended. As Corrie's father said, "If I die in prison, it will be an honor to have given my life for God's ancient people."

Eventually the ten Booms were betrayed and arrested—and, after only ten days of imprisonment, Cornelius ten Boom died at the age of eighty-four. Corrie and her sister Betsie were then transported to the Ravensbruck concentration camp. There they faced the "deepest hell man can create" but they never lost their bright confidence in a God of joy and love. Betsie died in the camp in 1944; a short time later, Corrie was released through a clerical error.

After her release Corrie embarked on a new phase in her life. She traveled around the world, a "tramp for the Lord," spreading the lesson she and Betsie had learned at Ravensbruck: "There is no pit so deep that the love of Jesus Christ is not deeper still."

Her experience of God was real and practical, yet amazing and miraculous—and because her faith had flourished in the midst of the cold reality of a concentration camp, few could dismiss her message. Her ministry of forgiveness and love was worldwide, and it crossed over the normal barriers that Christians so often erect between themselves.

"Consider the hands of Christ," Corrie wrote, "hands that are aching to take our own and guide us in ways that are good for us; skillful hands, worthy of our trust and love. Let us let Him clasp our hands a little tighter, and trust Him a little more than ever before— that our paths may be straighter and gladder than in the past. Let us make time for prayer, so that we increase the pressure of that hand on ours. . . . When we, tired and spent, lay down the work done in our own strength, our great Master will. . .remove every stain, every blemish, every failure from our service."

Corrie ten Boom died in 1983 at the age of 91.

RECOMMENDED READING: *The Hiding Place* and *Tramp for the Lord* by Corrie ten Boom (Revell)

A. W. Tozer
A Man of God

Keeping our eyes on Jesus,
on whom our faith depends
from start to finish.
HEBREWS 12:2

When asked to align himself with one denomination or another, A. W. Tozer described himself simply as a mystic. Christians from the Protestant tradition are not always comfortable with this word, but like Brother Lawrence so many centuries before, Tozer's mysticism was a practical kind that helped him experience God in the midst of the ordinary. According to Bible scholar Warren Wiersbe, a mystic is simply a person who "(1) sees a real spiritual world beyond the world of sense; (2) seeks to please God rather than the crowd; (3) cultivates a close fellowship with God, senses His presence everywhere; and (4) relates his experience to the practical things of life."

A. W. Tozer was born at the end of the nineteenth century, an age when science was beginning to shake some of the ideas people had taken for granted for centuries. Consequently, Tozer grew up cynical about God and religion. Just before his eighteenth birthday, however, in 1915, he was converted to faith in Christ, and began studying the Bible and spiritual writers. Gradually, his cynicism disappeared, and although he was completely self-taught, he became a deep Christian thinker and writer.

While he lacked formal seminary education, Tozer

would one day pastor one of the biggest churches in Chicago. His many books are, for the most part, outgrowths of messages he preached. His preaching and writing had one thing in common: All brought people into confrontation with God. "Is God real to you?" he would ask. "Is yours a firsthand experience with Him, or a secondhand one through others?"

Tozer believed that many Christians know a great deal about God—they know the accepted vocabulary, they know the songs, and they know the culture—but they don't know Christ Himself. Being Christ's follower does not mean belonging to a particular culture, though, just as Hudson Taylor taught in the mission field of China. Following Christ means being taught by Christ, and Christ alone.

Tozer never owned an automobile or lived the life of a wealthy person, despite his success as an author and speaker. He gave away most of his money to those who were in need, never allowing himself to be absorbed into the culture of his day. His tombstone bore only a few words: "A. W. Tozer—A Man of God." He died in 1963.

As Tozer wrote, "God discovers Himself to babes, and hides Himself in thick darkness from the wise and the prudent. We must simplify our approach to Him. We must strip down to essentials and they will be found to be blessedly few."

RECOMMENDED READING: *The Pursuit of God* and *The Knowledge of the Holy* by A. W. Tozer and *A. W. Tozer, A Twentieth-Century Prophet* by F. J. Fant (Christian Publications)

JOHN WESLEY
A MAN WHO "OFFERED CHRIST"

This is the message
we have heard from the beginning:
We should love one another.
1 JOHN 3:11

Like those profiled in this book, John Wesley focused his life on Jesus Christ. As the founder of Methodism, John Wesley endorsed certain "methods" of holiness, disciplines that would help Christians to be in right relation to God. But Wesley, like Luther, did not put his trust in works; he had been saved by grace. Over and over he reminded his followers that the way of Christ can be summed up in a single word: love.

John Wesley was born in Epworth, Lincolnshire, in 1703. His father, Samuel, was the rector of a Church of England parish, though both Samuel and his wife Susannah had been brought up as Nonconformists (rebels against the Church of England whose theology was closer to the Puritans' Calvinism). These contradictory points of view would eventually find a new and fresh synthesis within Wesley's theology.

As a boy, Wesley was the last of the family to be rescued from the fire that destroyed the Epworth rectory. Later in life he would refer to himself as "a brand plucked out of the burning" (Amos 4:11), so convinced was he that his life had been saved to fulfill a special vocation for God. Not until he was twenty-two, however, and a student at Oxford did Wesley begin to consider a serious commitment to God. Like Augustine centuries before and C. S. Lewis 200 years later, Wesley was an avid scholar and reader. As He did with Lewis, God used books to bring Wesley to the place where He wanted him.

The first of three books that particularly influenced John Wesley was *The Imitation of Christ* by Thomas à Kempis. Through this book Wesley began to see "that true religion was seated in the heart." He "began to aim at, and pray for, inward holiness."

From the second book, Jeremy Taylor's *Holy Living and Holy Dying,* Wesley learned about humility and a repentant spirit. He put Taylor's thoughts to practice in a plan for living or "rule." Such a plan would eventually evolve into Wesley's "methods for holiness."

The last book that particularly affected Wesley's spiritual life was William Law's *A Serious Call to a Devout and Holy Life*. This, wrote Wesley, "convinced me more than ever of the absolute impossibility of being half a Christian." He committed himself, through the power of grace, to being "all devoted to God—to give Him all my soul, my body, and my substance." As a result, he said, "The light flowed in so mightily upon my soul that everything appeared in a new view." Like John Bunyan and Fanny Crosby, and like the apostle Paul, John Wesley was changed forever by God's amazing brilliant light.

Susannah Wesley, John's mother, corresponded with her son regularly about all his new thoughts. Susannah was an unusual woman for her day, for she was not only well-educated and well-read, but also strong-minded and able to defend her ideas. Her influence shaped John Wesley spiritually and intellectually, and perhaps because of her, Methodism has historically allowed women to be in positions of leadership and authority. Her love and concern, as well as her sharp mind, helped hone John into the powerful spiritual leader that he would become.

At first, though, he seemed to be settling into an academic career as a fellow at Lincoln College. When his brother Charles formed a group called the Holy Club, John's true colors emerged. Assuming a leadership role, John proceeded to change the club's focus from academics to spiritual commitment and practical Christian service to the poor.

In 1735, in the spirit of Christian service, John and Charles went off to the colony of Georgia as missionaries to the native people. The experience was disappointing as John came home sorely disillusioned, aware now that his commitment to God was incomplete. "I went to America to convert the Indians," he wrote, "but oh, who shall convert me? . . . I have a fair summer religion. I can talk well, . . . but let death looks me in the face, and my spirit is troubled."

This fear of death haunted him. And just as God can use our interests, delights, and natural abilities to bring us to Him, He also uses our fears. At the same time that Wesley was sinking deeper into despair and fear, he was also seeking more earnestly for a faith that was strong enough to bring him lasting peace.

Finally, in 1738, at a meeting in Aldersgate Street, London, Wesley heard someone read from Martin Luther's preface to the Book of Romans: "So let us conclude that faith alone justifies, and alone fulfills the law. For faith indeed, through the merit of Christ, obtains the Holy Spirit, and the Spirit makes our hearts new—exhilarates, excites and inflames it, so that it may willingly do those things which the law commands." Wesley felt his heart "strangely warmed." At last he experienced the peace and assurance he had craved.

John Wesley spent the next fifty years spreading the Gospel. His single-minded objective was to offer Christ to everyone, and he did this mostly through open-air preaching. He traveled tirelessly back and forth across England, keeping closely in touch with his converts. Profoundly concerned with the poor, he brought many social reforms to England, working hard to fight slavery and bring about better prison conditions.

By the time Wesley died in 1791 he had formed a new church, Methodism, as well as the holiness movement that would eventually give birth to several denominations. He also left a legacy of reform that changed England. He had truly "brought Christ" to many—and he had done this not only through his preaching but through the real and practical love that he offered to everyone with whom he came in contact.

"The heaven of heavens," John Wesley wrote, "is love. There is nothing higher in religion; there is, in effect, nothing else. If you look for anything but more love, you are looking wide of the mark, you are getting out of the royal way. . . . Settle it, then, in your heart that from the moment God has saved you from all sin, you are to aim at nothing more but more of that love. . . ."

RECOMMENDED READING: *Works* by John Wesley (Zondervan)

CONCLUSION

Although the men and women in this book lived amazing lives, the only truly amazing thing about each of them was their total commitment to Jesus Christ. Their openness to the Holy Spirit allowed them to be used by God.

The truth is, each of us has our own spot to fill in God's hall of fame. Each of us has a special function in His kingdom, a role that only we can play.

All we need to do is turn toward Christ, focusing our lives on Him and His love. His Spirit will do the rest.

Heroes of the Faith

This exciting biographical series explores the lives of famous Christian men and women throughout the ages. These trade paper books will inspire and encourage you to follow the example of these "Heroes of the Faith" who made Christ the center of their existence. There are twenty-two titles containing 208 pages each. Only $3.97 each! Listed below are just a few titles that are available.

William Carey, Father of Missions
Sam Wellman

Fanny Crosby, The Hymn Writer
Bernard Ruffin

Jim Elliot, Missionary to Ecuador
Susan Miller

Billy Graham, The Great Evangelist
Sam Wellman

C.S. Lewis, Author of Mere Christianity
Sam Wellman

Samuel Morris, The Apostle of Simple Faith
W. Terry Whalin

George Müller, Man of Faith
Bonnie Harvey

John Newton, Author of "Amazing Grace"
Anne Sandberg

Mary Slessor, Queen of Calabar
Sam Wellman

Charles Spurgeon, The Great Orator
Dan Harmon

Corrie ten Boom, Heroine of Haarlem
Sam Wellman

Mother Teresa, Missionary of Charity
Sam Wellman

Available wherever books are sold.
Or order from:
Barbour Publishing, Inc.
P.O. Box 719
Uhrichsville, Ohio 44683
http://www.barbourbooks.com

If you order by mail add $2.00 to your order for shipping.
Prices subject to change without notice.